YOUR WILL, NOT MINE

YOUR WILL, NOT MINE

A STORY OF SUFFERING, LOSS, AND TRUSTING GOD THROUGH THE PAIN

MARISSA SIDWELL

Charleston, SC
www.PalmettoPublishing.com

Your Will, Not Mine
Copyright © 2023 by Marissa Sidwell

All rights reserved
No portion of this book may be reproduced, stored in a retrieval system, or transmitted in any form by any means–electronic, mechanical, photocopy, recording, or other–except for brief quotations in printed reviews, without prior permission of the author.

First Edition

Paperback ISBN: 979-8-8229-1895-5

CONTENTS

Chapter 1: Suffering	1
Chapter 2: Why, God?	6
Chapter 3: Fear and Darkness	10
Chapter 4: Trusting When It Doesn't Make Sense	16
Chapter 5: Timing	21
Chapter 6: The Power of God	26
Chapter 7: Miracles vs. Healing	31
Chapter 8: Fervent Prayer	37
Chapter 9: The Devil's Lies	42
Chapter 10: Control	46
Chapter 11: Anchored Hope	49
Chapter 12: God's Promises	52
About the Author	65

CHAPTER 1

SUFFERING

I am going to assume that you picked this book up because you are facing a trial in life that seems impossible or unbearable. Maybe you know someone who is facing a season of trials. Maybe you have never read the Bible and you're curious to learn about God and why He allows so much suffering in our world. Maybe you're just a friend or family member who bought this book to support me. Regardless of the reason, I am glad you're here, and I am humbled to have the opportunity to share my story of suffering and the wisdom I have gained from it. Now, to preface, I am no pastor or Bible expert—I am just a normal twenty-four-year-old girl who has endured great suffering and wants to share the wisdom that helped me get through it and share the ultimate faithfulness of God.

In November of 2021, I was living my dream life. I graduated from college, I moved into my own place, I had my dream job as an elementary school teacher, and I was overall filled with the joy of the Spirit. Everything was perfect. I woke up with a smile on my face and went to bed excited for the next day. My journey of illness and suffering began when I was in class teaching my favorite kiddos when all of a sudden, I was hit with extreme abdominal pain. I rushed home, where I was alone and very ill.

Between passing out and crawling to the restroom, I finally called a friend to take me to the emergency room. This was the worst night of my entire life, and little did I know at the time, this would be my daily life for eighteen more months. As the doctors examined me, the results came back negative, and I was discharged three days later. As I returned home after a traumatic experience in the hospital alone, sharing rooms with other sick patients and being told by professionals my sickness was all in my head, I began to feel scared and unsafe. I was clearly sick; why didn't the doctors find anything?

That question remained in my head for the next year. I tried to continue my life, but I was physically unable to. I could no longer tolerate any food and began to lose weight and energy daily. I could not eat. When I did eat, I would get sick, so I was terrified to eat. I was living an absolute nightmare. After two months of wasting away in my apartment, I quit my job and moved back home so that my parents could take care of me. At this time, I needed assistance walking, bathing, and doing any normal function. For example, my mom would help me out of bed, place me in the tub, and then when I was done with my bath, she would lift me out because I did not have the strength to get out of the bathtub myself. I was drinking liquid food due to it being tolerable most days. My body was completely malnourished, and I struggled to get even water down. I would go in and out of hospitals whenever I couldn't swallow water just to get fluids to keep me going.

Each day I cried when I woke up because that meant I had to face another day. I would take a bunch of sleeping medicine to sleep because that was the only time I didn't feel anything. I traveled with my mom around Florida to see the best gastroenterologists in the state. Eight specialists later, I was told by all of them that my illness was incurable and that my only option was to use feeding tubes for the rest of my life. I wouldn't accept that answer. How could I? I was a twenty-three-year-old, perfectly healthy girl prior to this mystery illness.

Due to my diagnosis by these doctors, I decided to make the decision not to accept the tubes and to waste away naturally. Surely heaven is much better than this, I thought. Just as I gave up, my mom discovered a surgeon she insisted I see. I was hesitant, but the doctor said to come in that day, and mom had already packed my sleepover and medical bags. This surgeon ordered two more procedures for me. I was upset because I had already been through over fourteen procedures that were traumatic, but I agreed to it knowing that this could be my last shot at life.

A week later, my tests came back positive. The surgeon explained that my esophagus was essentially paralyzed due to lack of motility, the capability of movement, and that a surgery could fix it. Later that month, they moved my surgery up as my condition was getting worse by the day. A Nissen fundoplication was performed on my esophagus, which means my stomach was stitched around my esophagus, creating a smaller pathway and therefore allowing food to move through. My surgery was very painful. I was ninety pounds at this point and the healing process was very scary. I could not sip more than a drop of water at a time and eat soft foods for another two weeks. I didn't know if my body would make it and I spent each of those days in a puddle of tears from the pain and fear.

Two weeks later, I began to eat soft foods. I was thrilled at the idea that this surgery would fix everything, and I would get my life back. Unfortunately, this was not the case. Thinking I was healed by the surgery alone, I moved out, got another teaching job, and moved away from my parents. I thought this was the end of my suffering and everything would go back to normal. Two months later, as I increased my diet, I began experiencing the same symptoms again, this time losing even more weight than before. Again, I could not tolerate food, sometimes not even water. I could not believe this was happening again and all I could do was be angry at God.

In denial, I continued to push myself, trying to get my body to cooperate, because I did not want this to be happening again. I would go to the hospital for fluids every weekend so I would have enough hydration to get myself through work that week. After a full day of work with no food, I would come home and sit on my couch and lay all my stuffed animals around me for comfort. I would shake out of fear for my life, but at this point I was exhausted from fighting, and I just gave up. I was ready to enter the gates of heaven. The pain and sickness were so unbearable I would've done anything to go to heaven. I was now on my knees daily praying that God would take me home because I was more afraid to live than to die.

I was deteriorating. My hair was falling out, I was freezing, my lips were blue and cracked, my brain was a cloud of fog, my muscles and bones ached, and I could barely talk due to lack of energy. I was slowly dying each day. I was ready to go home, where I could pass peacefully in the comfort of my parents. I sat in my room and began writing goodbye notes to all my family and friends. I was ready, but God was not.

The next day, I was awoken by an excruciating pain in my pelvis. I had an ovarian cyst that had ruptured and sent me to the hospital (when it rains, it pours; am I right?). This pain was unlike any other I had ever experienced. All I could think was *of course* this is happening. This hospital visit was different, though. The doctors and I both knew I was in no condition to be living alone or working. This was my breaking point, rock bottom, complete darkness. After healing from the rupture, I discharged myself from the hospital to go to my job yet again, only to quit midyear. It was heartbreaking to leave the kids and job I loved and had become attached to again. I packed my suitcase and flew home. My parents were heartbroken to see how ill I was. I told them my plan and that I did not want to fight anymore, and I was ready to meet Jesus face-to-face. Being the most loving and caring parents, they continued to fight this battle for me without giving up. My mom stayed up late at night researching until she found a practice called Waterleaf Naturopathic Medicine in Asheville, North Carolina. She begged me to give it a try.

At this point I had no hope left but went to please my mom. I thought that natural medicine would include hippies performing a ceremony around me, but spoiler alert, I was wrong. Now this is where the blessings begin to flow. The doctors tested me and immediately discovered a dairy sensitivity, leaky gut, and celiac disease, an autoimmune disease that causes your body to attack itself when gluten has been eaten. This practice, in six months, changed my entire life.

In four months, I was no longer skin and bone but back to my normal weight. I was not only eating food but enjoying it. I began working full time again, I returned to exercising, and I had all my energy back. I owe these doctors a million thank-yous for helping me heal, but I owe God all the glory for leading me to the right people and providing strong support. Even though I endured what felt like hell, I can now step back and see clearly how God worked through it all and fit all the puzzle pieces together. I can see why He may have allowed the things He did, and why He did not give me the miracle I prayed for every day. I can also see now that even though I could not feel or see Him, He never left my side and was there with me every step of the way. If any of this resonates with you in any way, I am here to offer you the wisdom the Lord has provided me through the scariest and most hopeless time of my life, and I pray that whoever is reading this walks away feeling peace and more empowered by the Spirit.

Prayer: Dear God, thank you for the opportunity to share my story with the world. I pray for my brother or sister who is reading this book right now. I ask that you open their hearts to this book and that you speak to them through the words I have written. Whatever it is they are going through, and whatever it is they need to hear, would you speak your message clearly to them. I am only just a vessel. Open our ears to hear you and our hearts to get to know you better. We love you and we look forward to what it is you want to teach us today. Amen.

CHAPTER 2

WHY GOD?

"Why do bad things happen to good people?" This famous question ponders many people's minds.

Through my relationship with Christ and the knowledge and wisdom the Bible has given me, I would answer this question like this: God has given us free will so that we are not forced in relationship with him, but rather get the opportunity to get to know him personally and as a result choose to follow him because of our understanding of all he has done for us and how much he loves us. Because there is free will, we are presented with decisions and choices along our path of life. When we make a choice, there are either positive or negative consequences. If this choice leads to a negative consequence, it is not the Lord purposefully inflicting pain on you, but simply a result of our free will.

Praise God that His mercy for us will always turn our situations for good even when we choose the wrong path. Now, when we face a trial that is not a direct result of our decision-making, we wonder why God would allow it to happen when He is all powerful and can make it go away in an instant. This is where the real meaning of faith comes in—believing when we cannot see. When we are faced with a trial in life, we must understand that our faith and trust cannot change due to our circumstance, because there is a bigger picture we cannot see.

Remember, God is behind the curtain of our play, orchestrating and working all things for our good, we just can't see it. So, why is this happening to you? For some it may be revealed clearly later, but for others we may not ever get the exact answer. We are not God ourselves and only He knows. His will fight for us behind the curtain; our job is only to trust that He is.

When I was first admitted to the hospital, I remember the Lord pressing the book of Job on my heart for comfort. I reread this story and could see why. In the book of Job, Job was a wealthy and man with a large family. One day, Satan appears to God in heaven and God was telling Satan how great of a man Job is. Satan argued that he was only good because he had so many blessings in his life. Satan essentially asks God for permission to punish him to prove to God that Job would turn from God and curse his name. God agrees only if he does not kill Job. Later, Job ends up hearing his ten children, livestock, and servants have all died. Job then ends up getting ill with painful sores all over his body. Job wishes he was never born and spends his days sick and grieving.

As time goes on, Job is miserable and questions the intentions of God. God eventually has an encounter with Job reminding him of his character, and Job becomes overwhelmed and acknowledges God's unlimited power. God then restores his health, providing him with double the amount of property, new children, and a very long life: "After Job had prayed for his friends, the Lord restored his fortunes and gave him twice as much as he had before" (Job 42:10). This story shows us a blameless man enduring great suffering, beyond his understanding. Early in the book of Job we see the devil and God having an interaction about what would happen to Job. This shows us that there is always a "behind-the-scenes" to our story. Just like Job did not know why or what was happening, we don't know what God has planned for our life or what He is doing behind the scenes. Even when we cannot see, God is always working things for our good.

When I was ill, I started to doubt and question the intentions and character of God. I thought that I was being punished for a sin I had committed in my past or for a sinful bondage I was still working on but couldn't seem to break. I didn't understand why a loving God would allow for this to happen to me. What I learned was that our God is not an angry God who punishes his children. Ultimately, there is evil in the world, and with the power of God we are able to get through it. Thank you, Jesus, for never leaving us, and for getting us out of our storms.

Oftentimes, God allows suffering in our life to develop us into better people and to help draw us closer to him. When we are suffering and at rock bottom, there is no one else to turn to but God. Suffering causes us to focus our minds on the Lord and to seek Him for navigation through the storm. This connection to him brings us closer and ultimately strengthens our faith. Allow your suffering to provide spiritual growth in your life. Instead of saying, "Why God," try saying, "God, what are you trying to teach me in this season?" As hard as it may be, turn to God in your suffering. He will guide you and show you the way out. When we shift our mindset from Why to What, we allow room for God to speak to us more clearly. Every tough situation is an opportunity to grow in faith and as a whole. Slow down and open your ears to allow God's voice to whisper wisdom to you. Ask him to speak to you clearly and he will.

I used to be so afraid to be honest with God about my doubts, but as I began to grow closer to God, I realized that there is no point in hiding anything from him because he already knows everything we are thinking and feeling. God is not only our father, but our friend, so we can speak to him like one. Wrestling with doubts is a sign of great faith. It shows that you really care about your relationship with God and want to know his plans for you. Doubts are discouraging, but it does not make you a "bad Christian." In fact, in my opinion, it makes you a wise Christian. Be authentic with God and ask him to give you wisdom and give you clarity on the doubts you are facing. God does not change His opinion of people like we do, he will accept your doubts and show you clarity if you ask.

Prayer: Dear God, your plan does not always make sense to us, but we know that one day it will. We know that we may not know why things happen and why you allow suffering, but what we do know is that you will never leave us, you will strengthen us in the storm, and you will get us out of this suffering. Thank you for fighting our battles for us. I ask that you strengthen our faith and rid of all doubts in you that may be filling our minds due to our circumstances. We love you, and we praise your good name. Amen.

CHAPTER 3

FEAR AND DARKNESS

As my illness progressed, and I became weaker and sicker. My mental health began to suffer as well. I could no longer see even a glimpse of hope, and I was truly convinced that I would suffer for the rest of my life. God felt nowhere near me, the pain and nausea felt unbearable, and I genuinely wanted my life to end so that I did not have to feel pain anymore. My entire life felt completely dark. On top of the physical pain, I have for all my life suffered with emetophobia, the fear of throw up and throwing up. With this intense fear, living with a stomach illness that made me sick every day and every time I consumed food was my absolute worst nightmare. This then caused me to develop severe anxiety and panic attacks. My vision would blur, my hearing would disappear, and then I would faint every time I felt like I was going to be sick, which was every day. So, on top of the physical illness and pain, I was dealing with serious panic and anxiety due to my extreme phobia. I told my mom that the only way I could explain to her how I was feeling was if someone had a phobia of snakes and had no choice but to lay in a bed full of them each day without being able to escape.

As time progressed with no change, my mental health grew weaker, and I no longer wanted to fight the battle. I remember not wanting to talk to God or write anymore, except for a few times where I felt urged to. Now, I swore to myself that I would never share the words that I wrote with anyone, due to shame and fear of judgement; however, the purpose of this book is to be vulnerable in order to potentially help someone going through a similar battle, so I have decided to put all pride aside and share with you a few of the notes I wrote while in my darkest place. This first note is a poem I wrote immediately after a doctor's appointment where I was told once again that there was nothing that could be done for me.

God, please take me
Doctors, surgeons, "specialists"
Waiting rooms, more visited than my bedroom
Sick
138 pounds
needle in my arm, uncross your legs for bp, pull your mask down for temperature, put it back on
Symptoms, a never ending list
Doctors, you know what to do... right?
No, anxiety, it must be anxiety
Yoga, breathe, sleep
Here, here's a pill
Answers? No but here, here's a pill
pain, suffering, miserable
A loop, a cycle, one that never ends
Food, now my own worst enemy, what should be my source of fuel is my source of pain
Here we go again.

Doctors, surgeons, "specialists"
Waiting rooms, more visited than my bedroom
Sick
125 pounds
needle in my arm, uncross your legs for bp, pull your mask down for temperature, put it back on
Symptoms, a never ending list
Doctors, you know what to do… right?
No, anxiety, it must be anxiety
Yoga, breathe, sleep
Here, here's a pill
Answers? No but here, here's a pill
pain, suffering, miserable
My dream career, now gone
My dream location, now gone
Insurance, gone
Plans, all changed, no guidance, no money, no path
A loop, a cycle, one that never ends
Here we go again.

Doctors, surgeons, "specialists"
Waiting rooms, more visited than my bedroom
Sick
108 pounds
needle in my arm, uncross your legs for bp, pull your mask down for temperature, put it back on
Symptoms, a never ending list
Doctors, you know what to do… right?
No, anxiety, it must be anxiety
Yoga, breathe, sleep
Here, here's a pill
Answers? No but here, here's a pill
Crawling through each day

pain, suffering, miserable
A loop, a cycle, one that never ends
Here we go again.

Doctors, surgeons, "specialists"
Waiting rooms, more visited than my bedroom
Sick
95 pounds
needle in my arm, uncross your legs for bp, pull your mask down for temperature, put it back on
Symptoms, a never ending list
Doctors, you know what to do... right?
No, anxiety, it must be anxiety
Yoga, breathe, sleep
Here, here's a pill
Answers? No but here, here's a pill
pain, suffering, miserable
Skin and bone, still no answers, still no help
More tests
Drowning
Feeding tubes needed, but please no I'm too scared
Lifeless, fearful, stuck
A loop, a cycle, one that never ends
Here we go again.

Waking up to another day is dreaded
Going to sleep, the best pet of the day, a time where I don't feel anything
God are you there? God do you hear my cry? Do you care? God if you love me why would you allow this physical pain for this long? Why? Haven't I dealt with enough?
I can't
No more
Tired, weak, done

Just keep pushing says mom
Just keep fighting says Dad
You are strong say my brothers
Strong? Tired, weak, done.
Hope is nonexistent. Will it ever end? I'm convinced not
Depression
Mom, I would never hurt myself don't worry
God, please take me home I'd much rather be with you
Brothers, I would never hurt myself don't worry
God, I beg you, please make this my time I don't want to live another day with this pain
Dad, I would never hurt myself don't worry
God, please take me

Shortly after my surgery, I was still feeling weak and unwell. I felt that I was different from others since I had to be cut open in order to eat food, and I felt envious of those who were healthy and could eat without consequences. As I laid in my abdominal binder, or brace, which covered my five incisions, I felt broken, worthless, and unlovable. On top of these feelings, I began to experience symptoms of PTSD. I would get sudden flashbacks of previous procedures or times I spent in the hospital. Sometimes these flashbacks would be so intense that I could smell and taste different scents and flavors. I remember one time I had a flashback of an ER visit I had and I began to taste and smell the saline solution that goes through your IV. I started having nightmares every night regarding being sick or in the hospital. These nightmares would wake me up in a full panic and sweat and were difficult to snap out of. The PTSD became so severe that I could no longer sleep at night out of fear. That is when I wrote these notes:

I've been cut open
I feel like my body is broken and damaged

I feel like it's broken and only functioning by a thread but not whole or fully healthy
I feel less than in Gods eyes and my own
I feel damaged
I feel emotionally and physically traumatized
I feel like I've been abused and in hell
I'm hurt emotionally from all the physical pain I suffered
I feel like I will never overcome this
It all feels impossible

John 14:27 says, "Peace I leave with you; my peace I give you. I do not give to you as the world gives. Do not let your hearts be troubled and do not be afraid." God does not give us the spirit of fear. So, while the world and the circumstances you're in may be feeding you fear, trauma, and anxiety, remember that God does not give what the world gives. Turning to the father will result in an unexplained peace over all the fear that you're rightfully and understandably feeling. Feelings of fear and anxiety are not "wrong", but what you do with those feelings will make all the difference. Turn to the lord and exchange the fear and trauma for an everlasting, supernatural, peace.

Dear Lord, thank you for offering us peace in every circumstance. I pray that the person reading this now recognizes their weaknesses in this season and exchanges them for your perfect peace. Please wrap them in your comfort, love, and strength. I ask that you put a hedge of protection over them as they continue to walk through this season. I pray that you fill them with your hope and love which will give them the motivation to keep going. We love you and we thank you. Amen.

CHAPTER 4

TRUSTING WHEN IT DOESN'T MAKE SENSE

The days I was living in went by so slow. Each day felt like twenty-five. Now, I would love to sit here and tell you that my faith was strengthened, and I trusted God every step of the way through my illness, but that is just not the case. I was so angry at God. I said things to him I never thought I would ever say to my heavenly Father. I remember sitting in the bathtub trying to make it through each hour, crying and yelling at God in my head. "Why would you inflict physical pain on me God? Why are you allowing this? You know that this is hurting me so much, if you really loved me, you would not do this. You must not even love me God! This makes no sense and it's not fair. Please kill me now so I do not have to endure this any longer." Rather than fighting the fear and misery with the truths of the Bible, I sat in my pain and allowed my flesh to take over. I became so blinded by my physical pain I could no longer see God.

During this time, I remember waking up with zero energy to even get out of bed and brush my teeth. I was in debilitating physical and mental pain, I had lost all hope and became overwhelmed with depression. My stomach felt like there were knives cutting up my insides, and the nausea was so unbearable I would have traded it for anything else, and there was never a time of relief. I remember sulking in doubt about God and whether or not I even deserved healing. I was so angry at God and hadn't picked up my Bible in so long that I thought at this point, I am not a good-enough Christian to receive his healing. I knew in my head that I should turn to God in this time as much as I could, but I could not bring myself to even speak to him. I sat in bed each day believing that because I wasn't praying or turning to God, no way would he heal me. I later realized this mindset of a conditional and exchanging kind of love was wrong.

I'm not going to sit here and tell you to just trust Him or that He has a plan, which you've probably heard a thousand times. What I will tell you, however, is that suffering is hard, painful, confusing, and flat out sucks. What I learned through this process of pain is that trusting God does not always look the same. You may have difficulties picking up your Bible and reading, or going to church during your time of suffering. Give yourself grace; this is okay, and the Lord does not love you more or less based on your actions. This is the beauty of God: "For by grace you have been saved through faith. And this is not your own doing; it is the gift of God, not a result of works, so that no one may boast" (Eph. 2:8–9). So, before you go letting the devil lie to you and tell you that you are not a good-enough Christian to deserve healing from God, this is simply not true. The Lord loves us right where we are at, even if we don't feel it. The beauty of God is that his love for us is unchanging. So even when you're angry and cannot even speak to Him, He sees you, He hears you, He feels your pain, and He does not want you to stay in anger, sickness, depression, or whatever it may be

So, what should you do when you want to trust God in your situation, but you just can't feel him or hear him at all—He is silent? This is where the true meaning of faith comes in. As believers in Christ, we need to understand that our trust in the Lord cannot change due to our circumstances. Our trust needs to be anchored in our unchanging God. He is constant. He is the same God today as what you have read of Him in the Bible, whether you feel it or not. When life becomes chaotic and you want to trust him, but you don't know how, it's as simple as just talking to Him each day. You don't get points off for not reading your Bible that day. Even when you want nothing to do with him, speak to him. It could be anything. You don't need a long fancy prayer in order to receive healing, the Lord just wants your heart.

If you are anything like me, if it does not make sense logically in my head, then it can't be true. I lost all hope and trust in God after I saw eight different specialists who told me they could not help me and seemed just as confused as myself. If my tests were all clear and the doctors were saying I could not be healed from whatever illness I have, then that would be the end of my story.

I gave up after being told I was not going to make it. The beauty of God is that there is always hope, even in the toughest of circumstances, when everyone is telling you otherwise, and when it seems impossible. There is always a way out with God. He is more powerful and trustworthy than any human or diagnosis on this planet: "Trust in the Lord with all your heart, and do not lean on your own understanding. In all your ways acknowledge him, and He will make your path straight" (Pr. 3:5–6). If you grew up in the church this verse may be well known to you, but I want you to really analyze and dissect it. "Do not lean on your own understanding" shows us that God's power is way beyond our human comprehension. I promise you He has a plan no matter how impossible it seems. He has never failed us, and He won't start now. "In all your ways acknowledge him" tells us to just simply recognize that God is with us. Remind yourself to direct your attention to him throughout the day, even when you're distracted by your suffering. This can be as simple as just saying the name *Jesus*.

Often times when we are so weak and at rock bottom, we may not have the strength to pray to God. In this case, ask the Holy Spirit to intercede on your behalf, like this: "Holy Spirit, I do not have the words to say in this moment, but please hear my heart." There is so much power inside of you through the Holy Spirit and prayer that we oftentimes forget about: "The same power that raised Christ from the dead is living in you" (Ro. 8:11). So, acknowledge him throughout the day, and remember that the Holy Spirit is living within you. When you do not feel God or have the strength to read your Bible and pray, simply know that He is within you and fighting this battle for you. He is so worthy of all our trust.

During my time of suffering, I genuinely thought that God hated me. I thought that there must've been some sin I committed that He was punishing me for. I truly believed that he was purposefully inflicting this pain on me to teach me a lesson. This is not the character of God.

God is a loving father, who understands our pain and weeps with us. He loves us so much we cannot even comprehend it. Another aha-moment I had after my journey of suffering was that God never wanted this to happen. He did not purposely inflict this pain on my body. It dates all the way back to the book of Genesis. God did not design this world to be filled with brokenness and pain, but man made a choice to follow their flesh resulting in the world we now live in—a broken one, filled with evil, pain, and suffering. But again, the Lord did not create us to be filled with pain but rather, sent his son to die for us so that through Him we can have an abundant life, even in a world of darkness. This is why we need Jesus so desperately. The Bible says that Jesus weeps with us. He mourns over our sorrows and loves us more than we can comprehend. While you may have moments of blaming God or wishing this world would end, remember that He does not want to see you hurting and He will get you out of the battle you are facing.

Prayer: Dear God, thank you for being a perfectly trustworthy friend and father. We know that we can trust you with everything, and that you can and will redeem our story. Father, even though this doesn't make sense and feels impossible, our hope lies within you. When we cannot see God, show us the way, and show us the light at the end of the tunnel. Guide us along the right path and show us our purpose and your will. We love you, and today we give you our full trust. Amen.

CHAPTER 5

TIMING

Have you ever wanted something so bad in life that you did not want to wait any longer to receive it? Maybe it's a desire to have a spouse, kids, your dream job, or the white picket fence home. Maybe it's a financial or marital desire. For me, I have always grown up wanting to find my person and have my dream wedding and then start a family. It has been the biggest desire in my life that sometimes I get way too impatient and want to force something that is not there.

A huge lesson I learned in the past two years is that we can't rush God's timing and that the wait is worth it. His plan is far better than the plans we create and imagine in our heads. We must remember that there is a bigger picture, and that God is behind the curtain of our play, orchestrating our life, and working all things for our good. When you have lost hope for that desire you want so badly, rest assured that the blessing will indeed come, it is just not in our timing. This is a hard concept for me to grasp because I tend to want control over my life. I have always had this timeline set in my head that I would be married by twenty-five, have kids by twenty-eight, and live happily ever after. I even have a Pinterest board set for my wedding day I created at the age of fourteen. God's nos in my life have always brought me confusion, doubt, and hopelessness, that is until I got sick and the Lord revealed to me how important it is to be present.

I lost everything (or so I thought). When I first got ill in 2021, I immediately lost all the money I had saved due to medical bills; I lost my class that I was so attached to; I lost the classroom I worked so hard to decorate. I lost several friends, and I lost my dream apartment I worked hard to purchase. At this point I felt there was no longer meaning to my life. I remember crying at night because my students would message me through our class app, asking if I was okay and when I was coming back. Leaving them absolutely shattered my heart and left me feeling empty. Why would God take all of this away from me?

At the time, I was so consumed in grief over the things I had lost that I failed to remember that God would restore all that had been lost to me and he would turn all things for my good: "Then the Lord your God will restore your fortunes and have compassion on you and gather you and gather you again from all the nations where he scattered you" (Deut. 30:3). God makes a promise to us in the Bible to restore what we have lost and to make us whole again. He promises to turn all things for good—what a statement to rejoice about! The word *compassion* in this verse sticks out to me because it reminds me that our God is a God filled with mercy and grace, not a God who does not care about us. The Bible also tells us, "And we know that in all things God works for the good of those who love him, who have been called according to his purpose" (Ro. 8:28). Praise God for working all things for our good in exchange for simply loving him! Remind yourself of these promises, set them as your phone background, and write them on your mirror, so that each day you can read a verse that offers you hope to continue moving forward.

When I moved back home, I had a selfish mindset rather than being thankful my parents could care for and support me. All I could think of was the time I was losing being sick and miserable.

I felt that every second I was spending isolated, and sick in bed, meant that I was not getting closer to my dreams in life. I thought that I was never going to be able to reach my goals now that I was stuck living at home again in my twenties. I had been rushing my life each and every day and now I was forced to sit in bed for days on end. After I moved back home the second time, and was able to find a team of doctors who could diagnose me and help me through the healing process, I finally learned the importance of staying present. To add, my parents lived in a small country town in North Carolina where the nearest grocery story is twenty minutes away and there are more cows than people. Keep in mind, I was moving there from a busy city in South Florida.

When I moved back in with my parents, I was filled with negative thoughts that I would be stuck there forever and never get my life back. I began to realize during my healing process that even though my situation was not ideal, I had so many blessings I was choosing to ignore. I had two loving parents who were willing to support me financially and help me get back on my feet, parents who fought to find answers for me each day, sat with me when I was sick, wiped my tears, and provided comfort and support every step of the way. I also had friends and family praying for me each day. They prayed in their churches, small groups, and alone. They would also call me, send flowers, write me notes, and text me to check in on me. I could not imagine having to endure this journey alone without my parents or friends.

Once I started changing my mindset to being more thankful for what I did have, then God's supernatural peace and joy filled me despite my situation. I slowed my pace down and decided that I was no longer going to rush God's timing, but rather be joyful in the place I was in. I chose to spend quality time with my parents and enjoy the time I had with them rather than wait impatiently for the season where I would get back on my own and move out. Through the process of being present, I was able to grow such a strong relationship with my parents, focus more on my friendships, and overall, be in a slow pace of life, which brought me peace. When you have yet to reach healing or the desire of your heart, rest knowing that God already has your future planned and all you need to do is trust Him and, in the meantime, enjoy each day where you are at.

When I was sick, I did not know how I was going to make it through each hour, let alone each day. To this day, I still don't know how I did it and how I kept going. I constantly watched the clock, tracking the time of each day. When it was past 5:00 p.m., I would become slightly more joyful because that meant I was closer to going to bed. When I was sleeping, I felt no pain and so nighttime became my favorite. I would take handfuls of melatonin so I could fall asleep quicker and hopefully stay asleep longer. I woke up sobbing each day because I did not want to keep going and I did not want to take on another day of pain. I would lay in bed for as long as I could, and my mom would have to carry me out of bed as I was crying in her arms, just so I could face the day.

Every morning I would look up at my mom with crocodile eyes and say, "I can't do it anymore." I would grip her arms tight and beg her to make it all stop. Everyone would tell me that God gives his toughest battles to his strongest soldiers, or that God wouldn't give me more than I could bear, but I thought that was a load of bull. I could not bear what was happening to me, nor did I know how to keep going. In these moments, I had to try and remind myself that even though I could not tolerate the pain, God was fighting this battle for me. He was working things out that I could not see. He was fighting and pushing and planning, all I was responsible for doing was to keep going. I realize now that you just have to keep going, the blessing is going to come we just don't know how long it will take, but it will come. If you feel like you cannot keep moving forward, put one foot in front of the other, and crawl to the finish line if you must. As long as you keep moving and pushing forward, God has everything else under control.

If you need some hope today, let me be the one to tell you that the blessing is coming. There is and will be light at the end of this tunnel. You will reach the end of your suffering whether here on Earth or in Heaven with the Lord. When you do reach the light at the end of the tunnel is not in our control, but I can promise you it is coming. Keep moving, keep fighting, and do not give up because you have the most powerful King of Kings on your side, fighting for you each and every day.

Prayer: Father, I lift up my brother or sister who is reading this right now. Wherever they are in life, would you meet them right there? Show them a glimpse of hope in each day and wrap them in your loving arms. I pray that you can give them rest, peace, and help them to stay present in the season they are currently in. God, you know their struggle, you know their heart, and you love them so much more than words can describe. Would you increase their faith today and give them the strength to keep moving forward, even if they are crawling? Show them that there will eventually be light at the end of the tunnel and remind them that you will work all things for their good, according to your purpose. Father, we thank you for your constant love, support, and provision in our lives. When we have no hope, we know that there is always hope in you. Thank you for loving us despite our actions and situation. Father, you will never leave us nor forsake us. You are an unchanging, trustworthy, and miracle-working God. We love you, and even when we cannot see, we praise your holy name. Amen.

CHAPTER 6

THE POWER OF GOD

In the song, "Same God" by Elevation Worship featuring Jonsal Barrientes, the lyrics describe how God is the same God today as he was in biblical times. The lyrics say that he is still a healer, provider, savior, and all-powerful.

This song has so much power and truth in the lyrics. I think oftentimes we read the Bible and view it as a fictional history book full of children's stories or old tales and we fail to realize that the God in the Bible is the same God today. All the miracles and stories of healing and overcoming obstacles were not fabricated and those same miracles are happening today. In this chapter I want to remind you of the many miracles and stories of overcoming trials mentioned in the Bible. Rather than viewing these as tales or fictional stories, I want you to remind yourself as you are reading that God is the same today as he was in these events.

In the book of John, the Bible introduces us to a man who had been ill for thirty-eight years. He laid beside a body of water which had been rumored to have healing powers. The man could not physically get up to move into the water at the right time, but still he continued to try and lay beside the water. Jesus approached the man and simply asked him if he wanted to be healed. The man replied yes but he could not physically help himself up and no one was available to help him into the pool. Jesus then responded with a simple statement that gives me chills each time I read it: "Then Jesus said to him, Get up! Pick up your mat and walk" (Jn. 5:8). So simple, yet so much power and authority behind those words. The man immediately picked up his mat and was able to walk.

This miracle reminds me that we cannot put all our trust in doctors, therapists, or humans on Earth to help us. While doctors and therapists are great to still use and have in our lives to care for us, our main source of faith needs to be tied directly to the Lord above all else. This story also reminded me that no matter how long you have been in the battle you're facing, the Lord can and will still deliver you. This man sat ill for thirty-eight years and still received his miracle. Now, I am not saying your healing won't come for another thirty-eight years, but what I am saying is to not give up on trusting God even when it feels like you've been in the storm forever. Last, this story has taught me to walk in confidence of my future healing. If you are currently sitting in a storm, pick up your mat and walk. Walk with your head up in confidence knowing that you don't know how or when, but you know that your miracle is coming.

In John 11, we read about Jesus raising Lazarus from the dead. The chapter explains that Lazarus was very sick and states, "When he heard this, Jesus said, 'This sickness will not end in death. No, it is for God's glory so that God's son may be glorified through it'" (Jn. 11:4). In this verse, Jesus describes how Lazarus's suffering was going to be used to glorify God and his power. Whatever it is you may be going through, remember that He will not only rescue you from darkness, but He will use your story to glorify the kingdom.

Lazarus had been dead for four days as Jesus made his way to join Mary and Martha, Lazarus' sisters. When Jesus saw Mary, and the Jews weeping over grief of their loss, Jesus began to weep too. Jesus weeping with them in this story has opened my eyes to the fact that he cares so deeply for us and feels sorrow when we feel sorrow. He does not want to see his children sad. Jesus then approaches the tomb and says to Martha, who explained that Lazarus is long gone, "Did I not tell you that if you believe you will see the glory of God?" (Jn. 11:40). Then Jesus prays to God proclaiming his trust and belief in the power of God: "When he had said this, Jesus called in a loud voice, 'Lazarus come out!'" (Jn. 11:43). Lazarus then came out from his grave with strips of grave cloth still on him. Jesus's prayer to God to raise Lazarus from the dead showed the people where Jesus's power originated from. This power is accessible to you today. The Lord is ready to hear from you and wants to give you a miraculous story to later glorify the kingdom and reveal the power of God. The same God who rose Lazarus from the dead is the same God today.

In Mark 4, a popular Bible story, Jesus and his disciples travel on a boat leaving a crowd Jesus was teaching to go to the other side. As they were on the boat, a bad storm arrived: "A furious squall came up, and the waves broke over the boat, so that it was nearly swamped" (Mark 4:37). At this time, the disciples feared for their lives and noticed that Jesus was sleeping in the stern while all this chaos was happening: "The disciples woke him and said to him, Teacher, don't you care if we drown?" (Mark 4:38). This verse weighs so heavy on me because when I was so ill all I could say to God was, "Don't you even care about me? Don't you love me?" The story doesn't stop in the disciple's doubt. The chapter continues by saying: "He got up, rebuked the wind and said to the waves, Quiet! Be still! Then the wind died down and it was completely calm. He said to his disciples, why are you so afraid? Do you still have no faith? They were terrified and asked each other, 'Who is this? Even the wind and the waves obey him!'" (Mark 4:39–41). Verse 39 always makes me chuckle because I can just picture Jesus half asleep standing up, casually telling the waves to chill out, and just confused why everyone is so afraid.

This story has so many lessons tied to it, one being, replace your fear with faith. The disciples had Jesus physically lying on the same boat as them and were still fearful that the storm would kill them. Although we cannot see Jesus physically right next to us in our storm, he is still there just as he was for the disciples. If you are a victim of fear, remember that the all-powerful God is right next to you and will never leave your side.

Another lesson I learned through reading this story is just how powerful our God is. Jesus stood up and immediately wind and waves listened to him and became calm. If the Lord can calm a storm on the ocean, he too can calm whatever storm you are facing in your life. This storm caused all kinds of chaos and fear on this boat, yet Jesus was simply taking a nap. He was calmly resting while the disciples ran around in fear and worry. Do not be afraid and do not worry about the outcome of your circumstances because while you are running around frantically on your boat, Jesus is sleeping in the stern. He is not afraid of what will happen in your situation because it is in God's hands, and He is completely in control.

These three stories only break the surface of the miracles Jesus performed on Earth. Notice how Mary, Martha, the Jews, and the man by the pool of Bethesda were not known as the strongest people of faith, and they did not perform a work in order to earn God's healing. My point is, our God is a kind God who loves ALL of his children and wants to bring deliverance and healing to all that give him their heart. You do not have to be the picture-perfect Christian in order to receive a miracle or healing. God wants you to simply just come to him and allow him to do the rest. His love for us is not an exchange, it is freely given. Thank you, Jesus, for your never failing, unchanging power and love.

Prayer: Father, sometimes we do not understand your timing and plan for our life. We often become impatient and want things to go our way. Even though we may feel these emotions and think these thoughts, we rest knowing that you have a plan for us, and your timing is perfect. We trust you God and trust that you will make all things good and new in your perfect will and timing. Help us to trust you in this storm. Help us to fight doubts and hopelessness. Father, give us strength today and every day to focus our minds on you and release control. We know that one day we will be free from the bondage we are currently in and experience the blessings you have for us on the other side. We love you, and we thank you for your provision in our lives.

CHAPTER 7

MIRACLES VS. HEALING

Growing up, I was a perfectionist in every aspect of my life. This led to an eating disorder at the early age of twelve. I struggled with an eating disorder for years to come and could never break free from the bondage of perfectionism. That is, until I met the Lord and gave my heart to him in my junior year of college. After I read the Bible for the first time, I was amazed at how much God loved me despite my past and was amazed at the miraculous works He had done. With this knowledge, I thought, why couldn't he do the same for me? I realized that He could, and He wanted to!

As I grew deeper in prayer, I became closer and closer to God. I could feel him and feel my soul on fire. I felt the Holy Spirit telling me He was ready to deliver me once and for all from this battle in my mind, and I felt that he was encouraging me to tell my small group about my current struggle. The next day, as my small group met at church, I told them about what I had been dealing with. I was so nervous to tell them because I didn't want people to judge me or think I had an eating disorder due to insecurities, however, as I spoke the words, I felt a rush of comfort and support from my friends. They immediately laid hands on me and prayed for a miracle. During this prayer, I felt an overwhelming peace, and I can't explain it, but I just knew God had healed me right there in that moment. The next day, I woke up and felt like I had a completely different brain. I no longer thought about food the way I did prior to the prayer, and I could not even remember the way I thought before. I was renewed and it was a miracle. This experience showed me that God is a miracle-working God yesterday, today, and forever.

While God performs miracles, He also allows for times of healing. The difference between a miracle and healing is that a miracle is instant, and healing happens over a period of time, but both are orchestrated by the Lord. There may be many reasons why God allows suffering and does not give you the miracle you have been praying for. There are lessons that can be taught, and strength that can be increased during these times. God may be trying to put you in a different place, or prepare you for what He knows will be coming in your future. When you are praying for a miracle and the Lord is not giving you that miracle, he is not ignoring you and is still working all things for your good. There is always a bigger picture that we cannot see and work that God is doing that we are unaware of. Whether we receive a miracle or healing is up to him, not us. This can cause us to feel out of control and trust God less; however, we must remember that our time will come where we will be healed by the Lord whether on Earth or in heaven. It is His will, not ours.

When I was ill, I prayed for a miracle over and over. I would put anointing oil on my own head, go to different pastors and ask them to pray over me, and cry out to God to heal me instantly. After these prayers, my circumstances did not change, leaving me so disappointed. He gave me a miracle before, so I know He is able. Why is He not giving me a miracle now? I was so determined to get instant gratification and relief from my pain that I begged God for a miracle. I did not want to go another minute with this pain and nausea. I could not bear it and did not know how I was going to make it further without a miracle.

This, unfortunately, was not God's plan for me. At the time, I did not understand this and became furious with God. I believe He hated me and wanted me to suffer, simply because He wasn't giving me a miracle. Now, stepping back after being healed and seeing more clearly, I understand that the Lord was strengthening my faith, and placing me in a different environment that He wanted me to be in. Without this illness I would not be living in North Carolina where I am now happiest, and without this illness I would not understand the things I do now about God. Prior to this sickness, my view of the Lord was very skewed and my love for Him was conditional.

Today, I am where God wants me to be, and am continuously working toward the woman God wants me to be. I know how to rest now, slow life down, appreciate everything and everyone I have, and overall, I am filled with the joy of the spirit. While this illness was traumatic and nothing short of hell for me, I do not regret it because of the person this experience created me to be. I also know that my story can hopefully one day help someone else and help to advance the kingdom of heaven. Do not give up in your battle because when you finally make it to the other side you will see how the puzzle pieces fell together and you will clearly see the positives that came out of your experience. While I may not ever fully understand why I had to endure the battle I did, I can see now why the Lord wanted me to go through a process of healing rather than a miracle because of all the things I learned through the process.

As I grew weaker and weaker, I knew that if my circumstances did not change, I was going to die soon. I became so desperate I would've done anything to be healed. I was so terrified and so sick of feeling miserable that I decided to one day drive from Orlando to Boca Raton Florida to see one of my favorite pastors, David Shaffer, and ask him to pray over me. I thought that if God saw my act of faith, then surely, he would heal me that day.

As I arrived at the church, I could barely make it through the service. I was dizzy, pale, freezing, and completely exhausted. When the service was over, I made my way to the altar to meet him and a friend of his who had gone through a similar health experience. They anointed me with oil and prayed the most passionate and strong prayer I have ever heard. The feeling of their hands on my back while praying for me was so peaceful and comforting, I could not help but break down in tears. I was so inspired by their powerful prayer over me, I left in complete confidence that God was going to bring me a miracle.

As I left that day, I continued to check for any signs of healing, as if I just spoke to a genie and he granted me a wish. I had the mindset that since their prayer was so powerful, I was guaranteed a miracle. Unfortunately, we do not get to choose our story or how our healing comes about. This was the side of me that so badly wanted to control things myself, rather than trusting in God's plan. While you may be praying for a miracle, it is not up to us when that happens. Walk in expectation that it will, because He will answer your prayers, but it will be the way that God has it planned for you, not the way you want it to happen. Healing may come when you least expect it, so continue to walk in the confidence and expectation.

* * *

Peace, Patience, and Perseverance. These are the three P's that God laid on my heart fairly early in my journey of suffering while I was waiting for an answer from him.

Peace
The Holy Spirit had prompted me to rest and try to stay as calm as possible during my season of chaos, fear, and the unknown. Due to my circumstances, the only way I would be able to experience peace is through prayer, listening to worship songs, and casting all

my fears to the Lord. The Bible says, "Do not be anxious about anything, but in every situation, by prayer and petition, with thanksgiving, present your requests to God. And the peace of God, which transcends all understanding, will guard your hearts and your minds in Christ Jesus" (Phil. 4:6–7).

When you are anxious and worried, try picturing yourself packaging up all your fears in a box and handing it to the Lord. He will trade these fears and worries for peace.

Patience
While I was suffering, I genuinely thought that it was never going to end. I began having thoughts about my purpose on Earth that I never imagined myself ever thinking. Each day felt like a never-ending cycle of torture, fear, and hopelessness. Although I could hardly hear God at the time, I did feel him telling me to stay patient. I was not sure if God would give me a miracle, or even heal me, but I did know that he wanted me to stay patient for some reason. While being patient, as hard as it is, this is when we should strive to not rush God's timing and plan, and rest knowing that He is in complete control.

Perseverance
To persevere means to stay persistent in doing something despite how hard it is to keep going. The Bible tells us, "Blessed is the man who remains steadfast under trial, for when he has stood the test he will receive the crown of life, which God has promised to those who love him" (Jas. 1:12). One step after the other, keep moving forward, and the Lord will reward your great faith and strength.

Prayer: Dear God, today I ask that you fill my friend who is reading this with the motivation and discipline to pray and speak to you daily. Help them to hear you clearly and encounter the Holy Spirit during their prayer. I pray that you help them to be vulnerable in prayer and give them the wisdom to rebuke the lies they may be hearing. God, I ask that you overwhelm them with your presence and answer each one of their prayers. Help them to walk each day in expectation of your healing and God I ask that you deliver them from their suffering once and for all. Thank you for always caring for us and loving us more than we can understand. Amen.

CHAPTER 8

FERVENT PRAYER

According to the English dictionary, the word *fervent* is defined as, "having or displaying a passionate intensity," therefore, to pray fervently means to pray with every ounce of energy you have and with full confidence in the power of God. When you pray fervently, you pray with the knowledge of what our God is capable of doing. Praying fervently may consist of getting on your hands and knees, crying out to God, and using the armor of his promises to shield you from the evil one. Fervent prayer is not just throwing up a request to God in hopes that he will fulfill that request, but rather, understanding that the power of the Holy Spirit is within you, and understanding that you are in the presence of the Almighty at that very moment.

At the very beginning of my illness, I cried out to God day and night for rescue. I put my faith in him and knew he was the only one who could save me from whatever was going on in my body. I got on my hands and knees, I worshipped and prayed in my hospital bed, and I read scripture to help me through the night. I remember sobbing in the hospital bed through each night, terrified of what was to come, as my roommate, Tracy, consoled me as I softly sang and played worship music in our room. I didn't know what my future held but I knew God was in control. After the second month of being sick and making no progress, I began to pray less and less until finally I had stopped praying altogether. My circumstances were not changing, so in my mind I believed that He could not hear me, that I was wasting my time asking him for help, or that he just didn't want to heal me. I gave up quickly after realizing that my circumstances were most likely not going to change for a long time. My peace instantly turned to anger and my hope into hopelessness. This is when I realized that my relationship with the Lord was unhealthy.

I based my love for the Lord purely on how good my circumstances were, and treated him as a wishing well where I would ask him for favors, but the minute I didn't get my way or something went wrong, he was no longer a "good" God in my eyes. This experience has strengthened my understanding of who God is, and what my role in pursuing a relationship with Him is. God is a king, a father, and a friend. We serve Him because of the sacrifice, grace, and mercy He has and continues to offer us each day. This lovely exchange is not based on force, but rather free will. When you begin to understand the endless love, protection, and provision God has for you in all seasons of your life, no matter your circumstances, notice your joy, peace, and prayer life juristically change in a positive way.

Matthew 14:23 says, "After he had dismissed them, he went up on a mountainside by himself to pray. Later that night, he was there alone." In this verse we see that Jesus had separated himself from the disciples to pray to God. The Bible also tells us, "And when you pray, do not be like the hypocrites, for they love to pray standing in the synagogues and on the street corners to be seen by others. Truly I tell you, they have received their reward in full. But when you pray, go into your room, close the door and pray to your Father, who is unseen. Then your father, who sees what is done in secret, will reward you. And when you pray, do not keep on babbling like pagans, for they think they will be heard because of their many words. Do not be like them, for your Father knows what you need before you ask him" (Matt. 6:5–8).

These verses give us direction in how to pray. First, God tells us how we should pray in solitude. This is because prayer is not to flash and prove to everyone that you love Jesus. Now, God is not saying never pray in front of anyone because there are many situations where it is great to pray in front of others, with others, and for others. What God is telling us is that fervent prayer should be an intimate moment where you are connecting and getting in the presence of the holy one. A time where you understand that the Lord is sitting right in front of you as you bring your needs.

The chapter goes on to say that we shouldn't babble and drag on our prayer because God already knows what we are going to say and what we need. Well, if God already knows then why should we even pray? What's the point? This is the question I battled with throughout my illness, and a question that ultimately resulted in the complete stop of prayer in my life. Prayer is not for God to know what we need, he is omniscient; prayer is to keep us connected to God, to get us in the direct presence of God, and to fight the enemies attack with the truth of the Bible. Getting in the presence of God through prayer will strengthen you, offer instant supernatural peace, and provide hope. Through consistent prayer we can also begin to hear and recognize the voice of God more distinctively. While you're weary and broken down during your suffering, please do not stop speaking to God and connecting with the Holy Spirit. The power of prayer will give you all the tools and armor you need to continue your journey.

What if I am angry, frustrated, or sad? How am I supposed to pray when I don't want anything to do with God? The book of Psalms is a book in the Bible full of lamentations and vivid explanations of people's raw emotions through prayer and song. I would encourage you to read a few chapters to see just how vulnerable and honest these prayers were. Psalm 13:1–2 says, "How long, Lord? Will you forget me forever? How long will you hide your face from me? How long must I wrestle with my thoughts and day after day have sorrow in my heart? How long will my enemy triumph over me?"

In these verses, David is crying out to God asking him how long he would have to endure his suffering. He does not walk on eggshells and say, "God you are great, and I am so happy to be feeling pain right now." David is truthful with God on how he feels, and this is called lamenting. According to Merriam-Webster lament means, a passionate expression of grief or sorrow. After he laments to God, he then follows by saying, "But I trust in your unfailing love; my heart rejoices in your salvation. I will sing the Lord's praise, for he has been good to me" (Psalm 13:5–6).

Here we see David pour out his frustration and confusion with his situation, then he rebukes the lies with the truth that God is unfailing and good. David shows us a great example of lamenting and the power behind it. The Lord knows how you're really feeling, and he wants you to express that to him. He doesn't want you to come to him pretending that everything is fine, and you feel great. God wants honesty; it is part of your personal relationship with him. When you lament to God, like David, follow the end of your prayer with at least one truth from the Bible to rebuke the enemy and not allow those emotions of your flesh take over your mind. You can quote scripture. For example, "God I feel so alone and afraid but I know that you will never leave me nor forsake me." It can even be as simple as reminding yourself at the end of your lament that God is good, and He never fails. This shift in my prayer life brought me closer to God because I was no longer pretending like I trusted him when I didn't, but I worked through those emotions with him and was reminded of his truth.

Last, while fervent prayer is a powerful and helpful tool, prayer of friends, family, and even strangers is just as powerful, if not more.

There is such a comfort that comes with an army of prayer warriors beside you. While I was sick and not praying on my own, I am so thankful that I had churches, friends, small groups, and family praying for me constantly. I do not know how I would have gotten through this without the prayer and support from my loved ones. While it may be scary to be vulnerable and tell people about your situation, the prayer of others is so needed when we are suffering. God designed us to be in relation with others, and he created the church so that we stay unified and support one another. It is so important to have people in your life who can pray for you. Galatians 6:2 tells us, "Carry each other's burdens and in this way you will fulfill the law of Christ." James 5:16 says, "Therefore confess your sins to each other and pray for each other so that you may be healed. The prayer of a righteous person is powerful and effective." When in suffering, I encourage you to be brave and let people in on your situation so that they may pray for you. The Bible tells us that other people praying for us has a lot of power and the Lord will recognize and reward your faith.

Prayer: Father, thank you for always being there to listen to our thoughts, feelings, fears, and requests. We are so thankful that we have a Father who cares so deeply about our desires. I ask that you give us the discipline to pray and passion when doing so. Help us connect with you intimately and block out our distractions while we pray to you. Help us father to come to you with anything and everything through prayer. We love you and thank you. Amen.

CHAPTER 9

THE DEVIL'S LIES

If I were Satan, I would aim to attack everyone's weak spots. I would put lies in people's heads so that they begin to doubt God and question his truth. I would put temptation in their lives so that they reach for instant gratification rather than long term fulfillment. I would want to take down every Christian so that they no longer trust and believe in God. This is exactly what the evil one does. As creepy as it may sound, there is a spiritual realm that we cannot see but is very much alive. There is a battle behind the scenes, constantly.

While God has already defeated the devil and gained victory, he is still lurking and striving to devour us. The devil places lies in our head constantly so that our focus shifts from peace to confusion. To fight this battle, we need to first recognize the lies. Some lies the devil might place in your head include: you are useless, there is no hope, what's the point, you will never reach your goals, healing will never come, you are not good enough, you have no purpose. When we recognize these lies, our next step is to stop and fight the lie with God's truth. Some truths may be: you will never leave me, I am good enough, I am a child of the king, God loves me, God is working things for my good, God cares for me, God can do all things, I am chosen. Rebuking the lies with truth gives us the power to fight

Satan and cause him to flee from us. Through Christ, we have authority over Satan, so we need to use that authority and confidently tell him to leave.

When we are in spiritual warfare, we have the option to either cower in fear, or be brave. It's easier to give up and quit trying, but when we recognize the strength we have through Christ and face our suffering head on, we will reap the blessings and benefits. God never promised us an easy life as Christians, but He did promise to always be with us, fight our battles, and give us the tools we need to face them. It's time to put on the armor of God, recognize that the all-powerful king is on your side, and face whatever it is that life is throwing at you. Do not let Satan fool you any longer. Rebuke him in the name of Jesus, and he will flee. God has already won the ultimate battle; Satan is only trying to deceive and torment you. Don't buy it.

I remember lying in bed, so overwhelmed with physical pain and exhaustion, that I did not even care to pray or try anymore. I was so done with God and my faith; I almost completely gave up on Him. I knew that the devil was filling me with lies, anxiety, fear, worry, doubt, and anger, yet I did not even have the energy to even fight it. This is exactly what Satan wanted. He had me right where he wanted me to be: angry at God, hopeless, fearful, and lethargic. When we let our flesh take over, which is exactly what I did, we become so blinded and deaf to God's presence and voice. We begin to drown in Satan's lies and lose all energy to even tread in the water. When you are in spiritual warfare, deny the feelings of your flesh, and continue to speak truth daily to yourself. Even when you are so exhausted of fighting, just continue to speak the name of Jesus. This will show Satan that you are not going to succumb to his tactics, and you will choose to continue to trust in the all-powerful God.

There are seven ways you can fight the enemy in your battle:
- Prayer
- The Bible
- Worship music

- Journaling
- Devotionals
- Christian Books
- Fellowship

Prayer provides a face-to-face connection with God. Through prayer, we can present our requests to the Lord as well as speak to him about our worries and concerns. He is listening intently and will answer your prayer. This close conversation with the Father is one of the most powerful ways to defeat the lies of the enemy.

The Bible is our tool for life. The Bible provides us with all the wisdom we need to know to navigate this world. Reading the Bible offers us insight, wisdom, and direct messages from the Lord.

Worship music is another powerful tool to defeat the enemy's lies. When we worship, we are reminding Satan that no matter what happens, we will still praise God, and He is the ultimate victor. Worship through your pain and allow the Holy Spirit to take over your mind and body.

Journaling helps us to speak to God through words on paper. This is one of my favorite tools because I am not great at getting myself to pray to God, but when I write I am able to be more vulnerable with him and release all my thoughts, worries, and fears.

Devotionals allow God to speak to us through small passages. If you struggle with reading your Bible directly, consider reading a devotional each morning to see what God wants to tell you or teach you. Books offer the same wisdom and messages from the Lord that God may be trying to reach you with.

Finally, fellowship is a very important key to fighting the devil's lies. We cannot, nor were we meant to, go through life's struggles on our own. It is important to have people in your life that can pray for you and with you through every season. There is so much power in prayer. I would encourage you to try using these tools, starting today, to help you walk through life with peace, power, and hope.

A prayer: Dear God, I lift up my brother or sister reading this and ask that you give them the wisdom and understanding of your word. I rebuke Satan in the name of Jesus right now. Whatever lies they're being fed, and attack they're facing, I declare the enemy to flee immediately. Through you, God, we have the authority over the enemy, and we thank you for that. The enemy is only a liar, and you God are a victor. I pray for my friend, for you to protect them from the enemy, and allow them to recognize and rebuke the lies of the enemy with your truth. Give them strength, motivation, peace, and hope today. Amen.

CHAPTER 10

CONTROL

Growing up, I was a perfectionist to the point that if I ever made a mistake, I would beat myself up for it for days. As a competitive softball player, this did not always go so well for me. I could go three for four with three homeruns, but still left the game mad at myself for not going four for four. In every aspect of my life, I have always strived for perfection and nothing less. This has been the biggest flaw and battle in my life; accepting that I am not perfect, and I am not the one who is in control. Learning to release my fears, anxieties, and worries to God has been the most freeing experience of my life. I finally reached a place of exhaustion where I realized that something had to change. Once I learned how to let go and let God, that is when I could finally experience true peace.

When I was sick, my perfectionist and control-freak side was tested heavily. Everything in my life was going smoothly, so this change in lifestyle was extremely uncomfortable and caused a lot of anxiety for me. How will I reach my goals now? How will I get back all the money I lost on medical bills? How will I meet my future spouse if I am stuck in bed ill? These are only a few of the questions that crossed my mind daily. I wanted control over every situation in my life, and when I felt out of control, that's when I was attacked with fear, worry, and anxiety. It did not make sense, and nothing seemed possible anymore. I felt eager to fix everything immediately and when I couldn't, I was left with no hope for my future.

As humans, it is a natural tendency for us to want to be in control of our own lives, but when disaster strikes and we have no control, we are left frantically trying to resolve our situation. As Christians, it is important to remember who is in control. We are not our own God. We have a heavenly Father who is in control of every single detail of our lives. So instead of gripping tight and trying to change your situations as soon as possible, recognize that God is the one in control and the one who will fight this battle for you. Exodus 14:14 says, "The Lord will fight for you; you need only to be still." This verse brings me so much peace knowing that my only job in this journey is to rest in the hope of God and trust him.

1 Peter 5:7 says, "Cast all your anxieties on him because he cares for you." In this verse, notice the word *cast*. When we cast something, for example, a fishing reel, we throw it far out and leave it there. We do not go and reach for it frantically, trying to grab hold of it again. This means that when we cast our anxieties and fears to the Lord, we should throw them far out to him and let him hang on to them. Do not reach back out for them and try to arrange them yourself. Allow God to hang on to all that you are worried about. He will sort them, and redeem you; all you need to do is rest and trust. Another example I once heard in a sermon is to imagine putting all your fears and worries in a box, sealing that box up, and leaving it at the foot of the cross. Do not go back for that box, and do not try to reopen it—just leave it at the cross.

Deuteronomy 31:8 says, "The Lord himself goes before you and will be with you; he will never leave you nor forsake you. Do not be afraid; do not be discouraged." God continuously tells us in the Bible to not be afraid because he will never leave us. He will always be with us! No matter what you are facing, the Lord is by your side, and He knows every step you will have to take, and He knows how your story will end.

Another verse that has brought me peace when I am trying to control my circumstances is Matthew 19:26, which says, "But Jesus looked at them and said, 'With man this is impossible, but with God all things are possible.'" This scripture showed me that even though I had no idea how I was going to get out of the mess I was in, God did. It also showed me that even though everyone told me that my circumstance would end in death, God has the final say and the power to change my circumstance. Release all control and notice peace overflowing your mind and soul.

I have never gained anything positive from trying to control my life, yet I continue to try and do it. When we put our energy into trying to put things in order, or make situations go perfectly how we want it to, we waste our energy and as a result become tired. Rather than exerting all of our energy on trying to control our circumstances, let's take a step back and accept where we are in this season, and box up our worries. Together, let's put our box at the foot of the cross and never look back. What a blessing it is that we have a God that takes care of every aspect in our lives so we don't have to worry. He is on your side, and he is for you. He will take good care of your worries and fears and make you whole again in his perfect timing. Never stop trusting him.

Prayer: Dear God, Thank you for being in control of our story. We know that we can trust you with anything and everything and that your plan is far better than any plan we could think of. I ask that you help us to release control and cast all of our fears, worries, and anxiety on you. We know that you will provide peace in exchange for our worries. Please release us from this bondage of control so that we may experience ultimate freedom in our minds. We thank you for your love for us. Amen.

CHAPTER 11

ANCHORED HOPE

The feeling that I may never be freed from my suffering was the most entrapping and terrifying feeling. I thought that the rest of my life was going to consist of feeding tubes and hospital beds. I was scared that I would never be able to work again, enjoy a meal, or go for a walk without passing out. I couldn't imagine a lifetime of this sickness and that idea so badly made me want to give up and speed up the process of wasting away. Some days I would not even try water or food because heaven sounded so much better than the current life I had here on Earth.

Looking back now, I am so glad that I did not give up. I am so thankful that my parents continued to fight for me and did not let me give up for good. If I gave up, I would not be here today, living this joyful life I now have. God has not only healed me, but He brought even more blessings into my life I did not know I even wanted or needed. I am now living in a state that makes me more happy, I am back at the job that brings me pure joy, I am living with a confidence in Christ I have not previously experienced, and I am living with the strength to get through whatever comes my way next. I would not trade these lessons and blessings for anything else.

No matter how painful my experience was, I am glad that I endured it because of the things I learned through it.

When I was ill, I remember my mom and I calling all the best specialists and making appointments to see them, telling them that it was an emergency and very urgent. Nonetheless, they still could not get me in for months. I did not know how I was going to wait that long just to see a doctor, but I did. As months went by, I would finally get in to see a doctor and I would be so nervous that I would forget to say something, and I was so desperate, I would practically beg them for help. My throat would get tight, and my eyes filled with tears as I tried to explain my situation. Every doctor I saw gave me the same response: "You have gastroparesis. You will need feeding tubes. This is uncurable, and there is nothing we can do for you." Most of them also told me that it was all in my head, and I should try seeing a psychiatrist instead. I left each appointment in ultimate rage and defeat. I believed every word the doctor said and ignored that gut feeling in my stomach that this was not the end. After eight specialists, and the same response, I felt completely hopeless. I felt as if my life was over, and I would never return to health. These lies in my head completely consumed me until I believed them fully. I was certain that this was my new life, and I was going to be sick forever. There was no longer an ounce of hope in me.

If you have ever been fishing in the middle of a body of water, you know that having an anchor is very important. If you want to stay in one spot to catch fish, you'll need to anchor the boat to prevent it from drifting away. The same idea applies to our relationship with God. We need to make sure we stay anchored to him, so we do not drift away from him, resulting in confusion, anger, and hopelessness. Without an anchor, we drift away from the truth and begin to drown in the lies of the evil one. Anchor yourself to the Father and allow him to directly provide you with hope through your trials. Do not drift from the Lord, and let the lies overcrowd your mind.

Keep God's word close to your heart, and you will make it through with peace, hope, and all the tools you need to keep going.

Just as God brought me out of the pit, he can do the same for you too. Whether you are a prayer warrior, or struggling to find him in this season, His love for you has not changed and never will: "Wait for the LORD; be strong, and let your heart take courage; wait for the LORD!" (Ps. 27:14). The Lord is coming to rescue you. He will get you out of this battle once in for all. He has a plan to get you out, and a plan for the rest of your life. Do not lose hope; instead, wait on the Lord! My friend, He wants to and will bring you out of the storm. Do not give up—He is not done with you.

Prayer: God, no matter how chaotic life feels, thank you for being right next to me every step of the way. We could not face our battles without you. Please continue to give us strength, faith, peace, and hope in our storm. Your plans are perfect, your timing is perfect, and your loyalty to us is perfect. We leave this book fully putting our trust in you, and confident that you will work out all things for our good according to your purpose. Allow us to use the wisdom we gained in our everyday life and walk with our eyes always on you. Father, let your will be done, not mine. Amen.

CHAPTER 12

GOD'S PROMISES

No matter how long you have been following Jesus, or how long you have been in the church, it is always important to go back and remember the basics—God's promises. According to Canadian school teacher Everet R. Storms, there are over 7,000 promises made in the Bible. Because God is perfectly faithful, trustworthy, and unfailing, the promises offer us confidence and hope in our future. They bring rest to the weary and hope to the broken. Meditate on these promises and allow the Holy Spirit to speak to you as you read them, reminding you that the Lord holds your future in his hands. Meditate on the following verses that are promises...

God Promises to

STRENGTHEN YOU

"So do not fear, for I am with you; do not be dismayed, for I am your God. I will strengthen you and help you; I will uphold you with my righteous right hand."

Isaiah 41:10

God Promises to

GIVE YOU REST

"Come to me, all you who are weary and burdened, and I will give you rest. Take my yoke upon you and learn from me, for I am gentle and humble in heart, and you will find rest for your souls. For my yoke is easy and my burden is light."

Matthew 11:28-30

God Promises to

TAKE CARE OF ALL YOUR NEEDS

"And my God will meet all your needs according to the riches of his glory in Christ Jesus"

Matthew 11:28-30

God Promises to

ANSWER YOUR PRAYERS

"Ask and it will be given to you; seek and you will find; knock and the door will be opened to you"

Matthew 7:7

God Promises to

WORK EVERYTHING OUT FOR YOUR GOOD

"And we know that in all things God works for the good of those who love him, who have been called according to his purpose."

Romans 8:28

God Promises to

BE WITH YOU

"Have I not commanded you? Be strong and courageous. Do not be afraid; do not be discouraged, for the Lord your God will be with you wherever you go."

Joshua 1:9

God Promises to

PROTECT YOU

"But the Lord is faithful, and he will strengthen you and protect you from the evil one."

2 Thessalonians 3:3

God Promises that

NOTHING CAN SEPERATE YOU FROM HIM

"For I am convinced that neither death nor life, neither angels nor demons, neither the present nor the future, nor any powers, neither height nor depth, nor anything else in all creation, will be able to separate us from the love of God that is in Christ Jesus our Lord."

Roman 8:38-39

God Promises to

NEVER LEAVE YOU

"Be strong and courageous. Do not be afraid or terrified because of them, for the Lord your God goes with you; he will never leave you nor forsake you."

Deuteronomy 31:6-8

God Promises a

PLAN FOR YOUR LIFE

For I know the plans I have for you," declares the Lord, "plans to prosper you and not to harm you, plans to give you hope and a future.

Jeremiah 29:11

God Promises you

AN ABUNDANT LIFE

"The thief comes only to steal and kill and destroy; I have come that they may have life, and have it to the full."

John 10:10

Prayer: Father, thank you for reminding us that you are true to your word and are unfailing. Help us to remember your promises daily and provide us with confidence knowing your promises. God, help us to use these promises to gain peace in our storm. Thank you for fulfilling these promises in our lives. Amen.

ABOUT THE AUTHOR

Marissa Sidwell is an author originally from Florida, now living in Charlotte North Carolina. She attended Florida Atlantic University where she majored in Elementary Education. Sidwell now works as a third grade teacher following her passion for teaching young kids. Apart from her love for writing, she enjoys going to the beach, going to the lake, playing and watching sports, and weightlifting. Sidwell's dream has always been to share her testimony to the world through her writing and inspire others to draw near to God even in the toughest of circumstances.

www.ingramcontent.com/pod-product-compliance
Lightning Source LLC
LaVergne TN
LVHW052003060526
838201LV00059B/3812